Pretty Girls Cook:

A Cookbook for Pretty Girls Everywhere

Author: Tamarrah Tarver-Small, PhD

DEDICATION

This book is dedicated to the Creator Jesus Christ, whom has given me the gifting to cook. Without him, my very existence would be null. I am forever grateful for the ability to bring happiness to people through my innate culinary abilities.

This book is also dedicated to my wonderful grandmother Catherine Smith. Catherine (Mamaw), you are the epitome of a virtuous woman. It is through your prayers that I have become the woman that I am today. Thank you for believing in me when it was difficult to believe in myself. I dedicate this book to you. I love you more than words can express! It means the world to me to know that you are proud of my endeavors. I am because you are. Your seed is blessed. Thank you for the many nights that you prayed for me. You have been my grandmother, best friend, prayer partner, confidant, and mentor. I love you and appreciate you.

ACKNOWLEDGMENTS

To my loving husband, Dr. Christopher Small, thank you for your support and love. You believed that I could fulfill the dream of being an author and I did it. Thank you for having my back in times of uncertainty. I'm so grateful to have you in my life.

To my mom and dad, Karen and Willie Powell, thank you for believing in me. I love you to life. I'm appreciative of the sacrifices that you have made for me. You have gone without so that I could have. I am sincerely grateful.

To my biological father, Stanley Tarver, thank you for being the reason for my existence. I know that you are looking down from Heaven and smiling. I know that you are proud. RIP.

To my siblings, Jervon Tarver, Ashlee Monroe, and Danielle Fennell, I love you all! Thanks for being supportive and loving. I told you all that I would take us to the top. LOL.

To my relatives, friends, and acquaintances, thank you for your enduring love and support. I am beyond appreciative.

I would like to acknowledge and express thanks to Rashada Houston for your amazing photography. To my hairstylist Thamar Williams, I thank God for you. Honey you rock! I would also like to express thanks to Nedra Whitaker and Jacqueline Flowers, for being a part of my book. You ladies are fabulous!

PRETTY GIRLS COOK

MENU GUIDE

Introduction 6

Pretty Beginnings: Appetizers 7

Pretty Eating: Main Entrées 17

Pretty Ethnic Main Entrées 32

Pretty Side Dishes 40

Pretty Sweet: Desserts 51

Pretty Refreshing: Drinks 64

Appendices

    Appendix A: Sample Meal Plan 76

    Appendix B: Entertaining Tips 79

    Appendix C: Basic Kitchen Utensils 81

Index 82

About the Author 86

INTRODUCTION

There's a myth that denotes the false ideology that Pretty Girls can't cook. I refute that mentality by expressing with action, the true culinary capabilities of myself and pretty girls all over the world. Not only can pretty girls cook, but we cook with grace, style, and with stilettos. There is nothing like a woman who can throw down in the kitchen. Whether you are a novice or a seasoned cook, this book is for you. This book includes both semi-homemade and homemade recipes. Most of the recipes have a Southern flare. The instructions are easy to follow, even for the most unseasoned cook. This book contains a concomitance of my most prized recipes. I have decided to release my secret recipes to you. Whether you are a woman who wants to make sure that your man comes home to a home cooked meal, or a single lady entertaining friends, this book is a novelty and keepsake for you. So grab your aprons, your pretty girl confidence, your ingredients, and let's get to cooking girls!

PRETTY BEGINNINGS: APPETIZERS

~Easy Breezy Meatballs

~ Flaming Fried Chicken Wings

~ Slamming Salad

~Sassy Sandwiches

~Bougie Baked Potatoes

APPETIZERS

Appetizers are the teasers to every main course. They give you just a little taste of what's to come. It's sort of like the kiss you give to your significant other before, well you know. It gets the eater excited about the main course. The key to an awesome mouth watering appetizer is to cook with ease and love. I know that sounds like a cliché statement, but when you cook with love, the consumer can almost feel the love put into your cooking. The appetizer should be light and should stimulate the appetite of the eater. Don't give them too much, but just enough to have them wanting the main course. Alright pretty girls, put on your aprons and let's get to cooking these appetizers!

"Compilation of Easy Breezy Meatballs and Sassy Sandwiches"

EASY BREEZY MEATBALLS

Ingredients:

16 oz bag Frozen Meatballs

12 oz bottle Grape Jelly

12 oz bottle Honey Barbeque Sauce

1 teaspoon Brown Sugar

¼ cup Water

- **Note:** This recipe requires the use of a Crock Pot.

Directions:

Pour bottle of grape jelly and Barbeque sauce into the Crock Pot.

Pour frozen meatballs into the Crock Pot.

Add 1 teaspoon of brown sugar and ¼ cup water into the Crock Pot.

Stir and let cook for 2 hours on medium heat before serving.

Serve meatballs on a nice dish.

FLAMING FRIED CHICKEN WINGS

Ingredients:

Vegetable oil (enough to fill ¾ way of skillet being used)

15 wings

2 cups All purpose flour

1 teaspoon Garlic powder

1 teaspoon Onion powder

1 teaspoon Paprika

1 tablespoon Black pepper

2 tablespoons Salt

Wing Sauce of choice

Directions:

Heat the vegetable oil in a deep fryer or pan on medium heat.

In a bowl, combine flour, garlic powder, onion powder, paprika, pepper, and salt. Mix the aforementioned seasonings with a spoon.

Sprinkle each wing entirely with the aforementioned combined seasonings.

Add wings one at a time to hot vegetable oil. Stir gently to assure that wings won't stick together.

Fry chicken wings for 14 minutes or until the wings have floated to the top of the vegetable oil.

Remove wings from skillet.

Place wing sauce (of choice) in a separate bowl.

Add wings to the bowl of wing sauce. Combine wings and sauce until the sauce is evenly spread on the wings.

Transfer wings to a serving platter.

SLAMMING SALAD

Ingredients:

One bag Iceberg Lettuce or Lettuce of your choice

1 Cucumber, sliced in ¼ inch slices

1 cup Small Cherry Tomatoes

2 cups Shredded Mild Cheddar Cheese

12 oz Italian Dressing or Dressing of your choice.

Directions:

Rinse lettuce with cold water as a cleansing agent.

Place lettuce in a large bowl. Add 2 cups of shredded cheese to the lettuce.

Chop cucumber in 1/4 inch slices. Add cucumbers to lettuce.

Rinse cherry tomatoes with water and add to lettuce.

With a large spoon, mix all ingredients together.

Add Italian dressing or dressing of your choice to the lettuce mixture.

Serve.

SASSY SANDWICHES

Ingredients:

1 loaf of Bread of your choice (preferably Italian bread)

1 tablespoon Mayo (or desired amount)

1 tablespoon Mustard (or desired amount)

Lettuce (10 Leafs)

4 slices American Cheese

2 tablespoons Olive Oil

2 tablespoons Vinegar

1 large Tomato sliced

½ pound Sliced Deli Turkey

½ pound Sliced Deli Ham

1 teaspoon Salt

1 teaspoon Pepper

¼ teaspoon Oregano

1 teaspoon Cayenne Pepper

Directions:

In a large bowl combine oil, vinegar, salt, pepper, oregano, and cayenne pepper.

Cut off the top portion of the bread. Spread mayo and mustard on bottom portion of the bread.

Place cheese on top of the mayo and mustard. Add turkey and ham onto the bread.

Place lettuce and tomato slices on top of the meat.

Pour mixture from bowl onto the lettuce and tomato slices.

Take top layer of bread and place on top of the sandwich. Cut sandwich into 8 pieces.

Sandwich is ready to be served! #Swerve in the Kitchen!

BOUGIE BAKED POTATOES

Ingredients:

4 medium sized Baking Potatoes

1 teaspoon Salt (per Potato)

½ teaspoon Pepper (per potato)

1 tablespoon Sour cream (per potato)

Bacon Bits (desired amount of your choice)

1 tablespoon Butter (per potato)

1 teaspoon Cajun seasoning (per potato)

Directions

Preheat oven to 375 °F.

Rinse each potato with cold water and remove any visible dirt with water.

Rub salt (a pinch) and Cajun seasoning (a pinch) on the outer skin of each wet potato.

Individually wrap each potato with aluminum foil.

Place potatoes in the oven and bake for 1 hour and 15 minutes. (*This may differ based on size of potato).

Take potatoes out of the oven and cut each potato in half.

Top each half of the potato with butter, salt, pepper, cajun seasoning, sour cream, and bacon bits.

Serve potatoes on a nice dish.

PRETTY EATING: MAIN ENTRÉES

~ Beautiful Baked Ziti

~Rocking Roast

~ Smacking Smothered Pork chops

~ Mushroom Chicken with Linguine

~ Brazing BBQ Chicken

~ "Catch It" Spaghetti

~ Queen's Pie (AKA Shepherd's Pie)

MAIN ENTRÉES

The Main entrée is the central meal that usually follows the appetizer. The main course meal should be well-planned, delicious, and should be the climax of all of your dishes. It's the main attraction. The goal of making the main dish is to satisfy the consumer's taste buds. There is nothing like observing someone enjoying the food that you have prepared. It's indicative that you threw down in the kitchen. Alright girls! Let's get back to work. Grab your aprons, your kitchen utensils, and lets cook these main dishes! Bloop!

BEAUTIFUL BAKED ZITI

Ingredients:

1 pound dry Ziti Pasta

8oz Mild Shredded Cheese

1/2 cup Ricotta Cheese

8 oz Mozzarella Cheese

Ingredients Continued:

1 Onion, chopped

1 small Green Pepper, chopped

1 pound Lean Ground Beef

1 32 oz jar Spaghetti Sauce (Prego preferred)

1 ½ tablespoon Salt

1 tablespoon Pepper

2 tablespoons All-Purpose seasoning (Lawry's)

1 tablespoon Garlic Powder

Directions:

Preheat the oven to 350 °F.

Bring a large pot of lightly salted water (pinch of salt) to a boil. Add ziti pasta, and cook until ziti noodles are tender, about 15 minutes. Drain noodles and place noodles back into the pot. Set noodles aside. *Do not place noodles back on hot stove.

On a cutting board, chop onion and green pepper. Set aside.

Place large skillet on medium heat. Add ground beef, salt, pepper, garlic powder, all-purpose seasoning, onions, and green peppers to the skillet and simmer for about 15 minutes. Drain meat in a strainer and return meat to the large pot that contains the ziti noodles.

Add spaghetti sauce to the pot and mix all ingredients with a large spoon.

Spray a 9x13 inch baking dish with non stick baking spray. Layer as follows: 1/2 of the ziti, mozzarella cheese, cheddar cheese, ricotta cheese, and remaining ziti. Top with mozzarella and cheddar cheese.

Bake in the oven for 45 minutes, or until cheeses are melted.

ROCKING ROAST

Ingredients:

2 tablespoons Salt

1 ½ tablespoons Pepper

1 teaspoon Garlic Powder

1 large onion, chopped

1 small bag Carrots (about 4 oz)

4 Scallions, chopped

3 large Potatoes, peeled and chopped

Ingredients Continued:

3 to 3.5 pound Pork or Beef roast

½ cup Brown Sugar

1 packet McCormicks Roast seasoning

2 tablespoons Worcestershire sauce

1 tablespoon White Cooking Wine

2 cups Water

- **Note**: You will need a roasting bag and a Crock Pot for this dish.

Directions:

Combine salt, pepper, garlic powder, brown sugar, water, white cooking wine, Worcestershire sauce, and McCormicks roast seasoning in a large bowl.

Using a fork, poke holes into the entire roast.

Place roast into a roasting bag and pour seasoning mixture over the entire roast. Set aside.

Using a cutting board, chop onion and scallions. Add onions and scallions to roasting bag.

Place roast in the refrigerator for 24 hours and allow roast to marinate in seasoning mixture.

After 24 hours, take roast out of the refrigerator.

Place Crock Pot on medium heat. Place roast and seasoning mixture into Crock Pot.

Peel and cut potatoes into ¼ inch pieces. Add potatoes to the Crockpot.

Rinse carrots with warm water and add carrots to Crock Pot.

Allow roast to cook for 5 hours on medium heat in the Crock Pot. Serve and enjoy.

SMACKING SMOTHERED PORK CHOPS

Ingredients:

4 Pork Chops

1 small Onion, chopped

1 teaspoon Garlic powder

1 tablespoon Salt

1 tablespoon Pepper

1 teaspoon Cayenne Pepper

1 teaspoon All-Purpose seasoning

3 tablespoons Browning and Seasoning Sauce (Kitchen Bouquet)

Ingredients Continued:

3 tablespoons flour

1 can of cream of mushroom soup (10 ¾ oz)

1 1/2 cups water

2 tablespoons olive oil

Directions:

Preheat oven to 350°F.

Place salt, pepper, cayenne pepper, garlic powder, and all -purpose seasoning in a bowl and mix seasonings together with a spoon.

Using your hands sprinkle each side of each pork chop with the aforementioned seasoning mixture.

Place a skillet on medium heat on stove. Place 2 tablespoons of olive oil in skillet. Place 2 pork chops into skillet. Brown each side of each pork chop for 3 minutes or until brown. Repeat this for the remaining 2 pork chops. Your total time of cooking each pork chop in the skillet should be 6 minutes.

After pork chops have been browned in the skillet for 6 minutes, set skillet aside.

Place water, can of mushroom soup, browning seasoning sauce, and flour into a 13x9 inch baking pan. Add 1 tablespoon of all purpose seasoning, 1 teaspoon of pepper, salt, garlic powder, and cayenne pepper to the baking dish and mix with large spoon until all ingredients are blended well.

Chop onion on a cutting board and place into baking dish.

Place pork chops into the baking dish and cover baking dish with aluminum foil.

Bake in the oven for 1 hour and 20 minutes on 350°F.

MUSHROOM CHICKEN WITH LINGUINE

Ingredients:

4 boneless Chicken Breasts

4 oz heavy Whipping Cream

8 oz Milk

8 oz Linguine Noodles

1 tablespoon Pepper

2 tablespoons Salt

1 teaspoon Cayenne pepper

1 Red Pepper, chopped

1 Green Pepper, chopped

8 oz bag Shredded Parmesan Cheese

2 tablespoons vegetable oil

1 tablespoon butter

½ cup Mushrooms

1 quart Water

Directions:

Bring 1 quart of water to a boil and boil linguine noodles for 18 minutes on medium heat. Drain noodles and set aside.

Combine seasonings in a small bowl. Season each side of chicken breasts with seasonings (salt, pepper, and cayenne pepper) and set aside. On a cutting board, thinly slice red pepper and green pepper.

Place stove on medium heat. In a large skillet, heat butter and vegetable oil. Place chicken, red peppers, green peppers, and mushrooms into the pan and saute' chicken and peppers. Cook for 14 minutes. Remove pan and set aside.

Place stove on medium heat. In a small pot, add milk, heavy whipping cream, butter, and cheese on medium heat. Add salt and pepper to taste. Stir until the consistency of the mixture is to your liking. Pour mixture onto your chicken. Serve chicken on top of your linguine.

Brazing BBQ Chicken

Ingredients:

6 Chicken Drumsticks

1 12 oz bottle Kraft BBQ sauce

2 tablespoons Salt

1 tablespoon Pepper

1 teaspoon Garlic seasoning

½ teaspoon Cayenne pepper

1 teaspoon Onion powder

1 tablespoon All Purpose Seasoning

1 Cup Water

Directions:

Preheat oven to 350°F.

Combine all seasonings (salt, pepper, cayenne pepper, onion powder, garlic seasoning) in a bowl.

Sprinkle (using your fingers) each drumstick generously with the aforementioned seasonings. Make sure that each side of the drumstick is seasoned.

In a 13X9 inch pan, add one cup of water. Add 1 tablespoon of each seasoning to the water. Add chicken drumsticks to the pan. Cover the pan with aluminum foil and bake in the oven for 45 to 50 minutes.

Remove from the oven. Coat each drumstick with BBQ sauce and place uncovered pan back into the oven for 5 minutes.

Take pan out of the oven and serve.

"Catch it" Spaghetti

Ingredients:

1 pound Ground Beef

8 oz Beef sausage

1 Onion, chopped

1 Green Pepper, chopped

1 tablespoon Salt

1 tablespoon Pepper

½ tablespoon All purpose seasoning

½ teaspoon Cayenne pepper

1 teaspoon Garlic powder

Ingredients Continued:

1 quart Water (for boiling of noodles)

2 tablespoons Olive Oil

32 oz Spaghetti Sauce (Prego preferred)

1 pound Spaghetti Noodles

Directions:

In a large pot bring 1 quart of water to a boil. Add a pinch of salt and 2 tablespoons of olive oil to the boiling water. Add noodles to boiling water and boil for 17 minutes. The salt keeps the noodles from sticking together. Drain noodles and set aside.

Season ground beef with salt, pepper, cayenne pepper, garlic powder, and all-purpose seasoning. Set aside.

Using a cutting board, chop onion and green pepper.

Place skillet on stove on medium heat. Place ground beef, onions, and green peppers in skillet. Cook meat until visibly there is no pink (about 13 minutes). Grab a strainer and remove meat from skillet to the strainer. The strainer removes excess oil. Set meat aside.

Using a cutting board, chop up sausage in ¼ inch slices. In the same skillet that you used to cook the ground beef, retrieve it and place the sausage pieces inside of the skillet. Cook sausages on medium heat for about 8 minutes.

After sausages are fully cooked, add ground beef, onions, and green peppers to the skillet.

Add spaghetti sauce to the skillet and allow spaghetti sauce to cook on medium heat for about 8 minutes.

In a plate, place amount of your choice of noodles on to the plate. With a large spoon, pour spaghetti sauce mixture on top of the noodles. Serve and enjoy.

QUEEN'S PIE (AKA SHEPHERD'S PIE)

Ingredients:

1 lb Ground Beef

1 ½ tablespoon Salt

1 tablespoon Pepper

½ teaspoon Cayenne pepper

½ teaspoon Paprika

½ teaspoon Garlic Powder

½ teaspoon All-Purpose Seasoning

½ Green Pepper chopped

Box of instant mashed potatoes prepared (follow instructions on box)

1 bottle of A-1 Steak Sauce

Ingredients Continued:

1 bag 8 oz Mild Cheddar Cheese

2 cans Pillsbury Crescent Rolls

1 small Onion Chopped

½ can Corn drained

Non-stick Baking Spray

Directions:

Preheat oven to 350°F.

In a 13X9 inch baking pan, thoroughly spray non-stick baking spray across the entire pan.

Open one can of the Pillsbury crescent rolls. Unfold crescent rolls and lay each layer flat on to the bottom of the baking pan until the pan is completely covered with crescent rolls. Place pan in the oven for 5 minutes.

Chop green pepper and onion on a cutting board.

Place a large skillet on the stove on medium heat. Take ground beef and place into skillet. Add salt, pepper, cayenne pepper, paprika, all-purpose seasoning, onions, garlic powder, and green peppers to the meat and cook for about 13 minutes or until there is no more visible "pink" in the ground beef.

Transfer meat from skillet to strainer. Strain until oil drippings are removed. Set aside.

Remove crescent baking pan out of the oven and set aside.

Using the 8 oz box of instant mashed potatoes, follow instructions on the box and set instant mashed potatoes to the side when potatoes are completely cooked.

Place ground beef back into empty pre used skillet on stove on low heat. Add A-1 sauce and corn to the skillet and cook on low heat for 8 minutes.

Take beef and corn mixture and pour into baking pan. Spread mashed potatoes on top of meat. Sprinkle and cover mashed potatoes with Cheese. Open up another can of Pillsbury crescent rolls. Spread unrolled crescent rolls on top of cheese until cheese is completely covered. Sprinkle 1 teaspoon of garlic powder and 1 teaspoon of all-purpose seasoning on top of crescents.

Bake for 45 minutes on 350 °F.

Take out of the oven and serve.

PRETTY ETHNIC MAIN ENTRÉES

~Jamming Curry Chicken, Shrimp, & Rice

~Chicken Quesadilla

~Beef & Broccoli with Rice

ETHNIC MAIN ENTRÉES

These main entrées emanate from other countries and/or islands. It's imperative that every pretty girl is eccentric and flexible in the kitchen. These dishes will have your consumer begging for more. They will be saying "Ay mon" give me some of dhat curry. LOL. On another note, it gives you as a cook, the ability to prepare dishes outside of the everyday American food choices. Let's get to cooking girls!

JAMMING CURRY CHICKEN, SHRIMP, & RICE

Ingredients:

6 Boneless Chicken Breasts or Chicken parts of your choice

2 cups small Shrimp, peeled and deveined

1 Onion, chopped

1 stalk of Scallions, chopped

1 Green Pepper, chopped

1 Yellow Pepper, chopped

1 Red Pepper, chopped

6 cups Rice (cooked)

2 Potatoes

4 Carrots

1 can Corn

2 ½ cups Water

½ cup Chicken Broth

6 tablespoons Curry Powder

1 tablespoon Vegetable Oil

1 tablespoon Garlic Powder

1 tablespoon Salt

1 tablespoon Thyme Seasoning

1 Tomato, chopped

Directions:

Clean and rinse chicken with water. Peel, devein, and clean shrimp. Rinse shrimp with cold water and remove the outer tail. Place chicken and shrimp aside.

Using a cutting board and knife, chop onion, scallions, green pepper, yellow pepper, and red pepper into small pieces.

Season chicken and shrimp with salt, pepper, garlic powder, and pepper.

Place chicken and shrimp in a large bowl. Place onions, scallions, thyme seasoning, red peppers, yellow peppers, and green peppers into the bowl. Allow the ingredients to marinate by placing the chicken and shrimp into the refrigerator for 3 hours. Make sure that you cover the bowl with saran wrap.

After the chicken and shrimp are done marinating, remove bowl from the refrigerator.

Place bowl aside.

On a cutting board peel and chop potatoes into small pieces.

Place stove on medium heat. Using a large skillet, place on stove. Add vegetable oil to skillet. Place chicken, shrimp, and vegetable mixture (onions and peppers) into the pan and allow the chicken and shrimp to brown by cooking chicken for about 14 minutes.

Add water, curry seasoning, chicken broth, corn, carrots, and potatoes to the skillet. Allow chicken to cook for about 1 hour and 15 minutes.

Serve dish wish instant rice.

Enjoy.

CHICKEN QUESADILLA

Ingredients:

Salt (1/2 tablespoon per chicken breast)

Pepper (1 teaspoon per chicken breast)

Garlic Powder (1 teaspoon per chicken breast)

Onion Powder (1 teaspoon per chicken breast)

4 Chicken Breasts cut into ½ inch pieces

1 can Corn (drained)

1 can Black Beans (rinsed)

1 can Salsa 8 oz (refrigerated)

1 8 oz Mexican style Kraft cheese

8 soft circle Flour Tortillas

2 tablespoons Butter

Directions:

Place skillet on medium heat.

Melt 2 tablespoons of butter by placing butter into skillet.

Season each chicken breast with salt, pepper, garlic powder, onion powder, and cayenne pepper.

Place chicken into skillet and cook for 14 minutes or until chicken is completely cooked (there should be no pink in the center of the chicken).

Remove skillet from stove and set aside. Place chicken on a cutting board and cut chicken in ¼ inch pieces.

In another medium sized skillet, place on heated stove (medium heat). Spray skillet with non-stick spray. Place one tortilla into the skillet. Add cheese, black beans, corn, and chicken on top of the tortilla. Place another tortilla on top of the chicken, cheese, and black beans. Cook each side of the quesadilla for 3 minutes. Repeat these steps for each quesadilla that you make.

When serving the quesadillas, serve with a side of salsa of your choice. I would suggest Tostitos mild salsa.

Note: Use 4 oz of chicken, 1 tablespoon of corn, black beans, and cheese for each quesadilla.

BEEF AND BROCOLI WITH RICE

Ingredients:

1 Green Pepper, chopped

1 Red Pepper, chopped

1 small Onion, chopped

Ingredients Continued:

4 Tablespoons Cornstarch

1/2 cup Water

2 tablespoons Water

1/2 teaspoon Garlic Powder

1 teaspoon pepper

1 lb Boneless Round Steak or 1 lb charcoal Chuck Steak, cut into thin 3-inch strips

2 tablespoons Vegetable oil, divided

4 cups Broccoli Florets

1/3 cup Soy Sauce

¼ cup tablespoons Brown Sugar

1/8 teaspoon Ground Ginger

8 oz instant Rice, cooked

Directions:

In a bowl, combine 2 tablespoons cornstarch, 2 tablespoons water, pepper, and garlic powder until smooth.

Add beef to the bowl and toss.

Using a cutting board, chop onion, green pepper, and red pepper.

Place large skillet over medium heat and stir-fry beef, red peppers, green peppers, and onions in 1 tablespoon of vegetable oil for about 10 to 12 minutes. Set aside.

Using another skillet, place skillet on medium heat. Spray skillet with nonstick spray. Add 1 tablespoon of vegetable oil to skillet.

Stir-fry broccoli in skillet for about 7 minutes. Take beef and place beef into broccoli skillet.

Combine soy sauce, brown sugar, ginger and remaining 2 tablespoons of cornstarch and ½ cup of water until smooth; add to the pan. Cook and stir for 2 minutes. Serve over cooked rice.

SIDE DISHES

~ Banging Macaroni and Cheese

~Boss Baked Beans

~Wild Out Rice

~ Slap Your Momma Cornbread

~ "Turn up" Cabbage

SIDE DISHES

Side dishes are dishes that accompany the main entrée. They give the main entrée' that extra oomph needed to make the perfect meal. Have you ever eaten a meal and said to yourself, "I wish I had a side of rice?" Well, that's why it is imperative that you have side dishes to go with the main entrée. Alright girls, it's time to cook pretty in the kitchen. Lets cook!

BANGING MACARONI AND CHEESE

Ingredients:

16 oz box Elbows Noodles

2 cups Milk

1 bag 8 oz Colby & Monterey Shredded Cheese

1 bag 8 oz Sharp Cheddar Cheese

1 bag 8 oz bag Mozzarella Shredded Cheese

Ingredients Continued:

1 block Velveeta Cheese (8 oz)

½ cup Ricotta Cheese

½ cup Butter

1 ½ tablespoon Salt & pinch Salt

1 tablespoon Pepper & pinch Pepper

¼ teaspoon Garlic Powder

¼ tablespoon All-Purpose Seasoning

1 Egg

1 quart Water

Directions:

Preheat oven to 350 °F.

Boil 1 quart of water in a large pot on stove. Add elbow noodles to boiling water. Add 1 pinch of salt and boil noodles for 18 minutes or until noodles are tender. Drain noodles in a strainer and set noodles aside.

Return empty large pot to the stove. Place stove on low heat. Add milk, butter, velveeta cheese, ricotta cheese, 6 oz sharp cheddar, 6 oz Colby and Monterey cheese, and 4 oz mozzarella cheese to the pot until cheese is melted. Place noodles in the pot with cheese mixture and stir generously. Season the noodles with salt, pepper, garlic powder, and all purpose seasoning. Add 1 egg and mix with a large spoon for 2 minutes.

Spray non-stick spray in a 13x9 inch baking pan. Place macaroni in baking pan. Sprinkle remaining cheese (Mozarella, Colby & Monterey, and Sharp Cheddar) on top of the macaroni. Take a pinch of salt and pepper and sprinkle on top of cheese.

Bake in the oven for 45-50 minutes on 350 °F.

BOSS BAKED BEANS

Ingredients:

55 oz can of Bush's Original Baked Beans

1 teaspoon Vanilla Extract

1 ½ teaspoon Cinnamon

1 ½ cup White Sugar

¾ cup Brown Sugar

1 teaspoon Yellow Mustard

1/2 tablespoon of Minced Onions

Directions:

Preheat oven to 350 °F.

Open canned beans with can opener.

Pour Bush's beans in a baking pan, preferably a 13X9 inch baking pan.

Add white sugar, brown sugar, vanilla extract, cinnamon, minced onions and mustard to the beans.

Using a large spoon, mix all ingredients for about 30 seconds.

Placed baked beans into the oven for 35 to 40 minutes.

Remove from oven and enjoy!

WILD OUT RICE

Ingredients:

2 pounds of Lean Ground Beef

2 cups Beef Broth

1 Green Pepper, chopped

1 Red Pepper, chopped

1 small Onion, chopped

2 tablespoons Salt

2 tablespoons of Minced Garlic

1 tablespoon Pepper

1 teaspoon Cajun Seasoning

1 teaspoon All-Purpose Seasoning

10 cups of Cooked Rice, Instant Rice

¼ cup Parsley, chopped

¼ cup Celery, chopped

Directions:

Dice and chop onion, red pepper, celery, parsley, and green pepper.

Brown meat on medium heat in a large skillet. Add salt, pepper, cayenne pepper, garlic, Cajun seasoning, cayenne pepper, and all-purpose seasoning to meat and cook.

Add red peppers, green peppers, parsley, onions, and celery to meat and cook thoroughly for about 15 minutes or until meat is completely browned. Remove from stove and set aside.

Cook instant rice. Follow instructions on the box of instant rice.

Pour beef broth over cooked rice. Add beef mixture to cooked instant rice. Allow mixture to simmer on stove for 10 minutes on low heat.

Pour entire rice and beef mixture into a baking dish. Place rice in the oven for 45 minutes on 350 °F.

Remove from oven. Eat and enjoy.

SLAP YOUR MAMMA CORNBREAD

Ingredients:

2 boxes Jiffy Cornbread

¾ cup Milk

1 stick Butter, melted

3 tablespoons of unmelted Butter (for greasing of the pan)

2 cups sugar

1 teaspoon Vanilla Extract

3 Eggs

2 tablespoons Flour

1/2 cup Sour Cream

Directions:

Preheat oven to 350 °F.

Generously coat baking dish with 3 tablespoons of butter.

In a large mixing bowl, whisk 3 eggs and break up the yokes by whisking for 1 minute. Add Jiffy cornbread mix, milk, sugar, sour cream, flour, and vanilla extract.

Place a small pot on medium heat on the stove and melt 1 stick of butter. Add butter into cornbread mixture and mix with a mixer for 3 minutes on medium speed or until all lumps are gone.

Place cornbread into oven for 35 to 40 minutes.

Remove from oven and allow cornbread to cool for 10 minutes.

Serve and enjoy.

"TURN UP" CABBAGE

Ingredients:

2 heads Cabbage

8 slices Bacon

1 tablespoon Salt

½ tablespoon Pepper

½ tablespoon All-Purpose seasoning

½ teaspoon Cayenne pepper

2 ½ cups Water

½ teaspoon Garlic salt

½ teaspoon Onion powder

Ingredients Continued:

2 tablespoons Butter

½ cup Chicken Broth

Directions:

Place medium sized pot on medium heat. Cook bacon for 11 minutes or until fully cooked. Set pan aside.

Remove the stem from the cabbage. Do not cook the stem part of the cabbage.

Slice cabbage into ½ an inch to 1 inch pieces.

Place a separate large pot on low heat on to the stove.

Add water, chicken broth, butter, salt, pepper, garlic salt, onion powder, cayenne pepper, and all purpose seasoning to the pot. Take bacon and bacon grease and pour into large pot.

Place cabbage into large pot and cover the pot. Cook cabbage on low heat for 30 to 35 minutes, stirring occasionally or until cabbage is fully cooked.

Add seasonings to the liking of your taste. Enjoy!

PRETTY SWEETS: DESSERTS

~ Prissy Peach Cobbler

~ Brilliant Bread Pudding with Bourbon Sauce

~ Stunning Sweet Potato Pie

~Tamarrah's Signature 6 Flavor Pound cake

~Who's Fake? No Bake Cheesecake

DESSERTS

The conclusion of every meal should end with a sweet treat. I don't care how full you are, there is ALWAYS room for dessert. The dessert that you prepare should be so delicious, so delectable, so tantalizing to the taste buds, that it makes the consumer ask for more. These desserts are a sure hit for any guest that you may be entertaining. Get out your mixers girls, we are about to "whip up" some orgasmic desserts! Leggggooooooo!

"Compilation of Prissy Peach Cobbler and Stunning Sweet Potato Pie"

PRISSY PEACH COBBLER

Ingredients:

2 cans of 15 oz sliced Peaches

¼ cup Pineapple Juice

1/4 cup Orange Juice

2 tablespoons Lemon Juice

1 teaspoon ground Cinnamon

1 teaspoon ground Nutmeg

½ teaspoon Vanilla Extract

1 tablespoon Cornstarch

1 ½ cup White Sugar

½ cup Brown Sugar

1 cup Butter (2 sticks)

4 deep dish pie crusts (rolled out and flattened)

- **Note:** Use 2 pie crusts for the top and 2 pie crusts for the bottom of this cobbler.

Directions:

Preheat oven to 350 °F.

Place saucepan on medium heat on stove. Place butter in sauce pan and melt butter. Add orange juice and pineapple juice to the pan.

Add lemon juice to mixture. Using a whisk or mixing spoon, mix ingredients together in sauce pan.

Add peaches to the mixture

Place white sugar, brown sugar, and cornstarch in a bowl and mix ingredients together with a large spoon.

Directions Continued:

Add cinnamon, vanilla extract, and nutmeg to the bowl with the sugar mixture. Using a large spoon, mix the ingredients together. Take sugar mixture and add to saucepan that contains the peaches. Mix all ingredients together by stirring with a large spoon.

Spray pan with baking spray.

Take 2 pie crusts and mold together into a large ball. With a rolling pin, roll out dough until dough is stretched enough to fit into a 13x9 inch baking pan. Place dough in pan and mold dough as needed to fit baking pan.

Pour peaches into the pan.

With the remaining crust, mold crust into a ball with your hands. Using a cutting board as your base, place crust onto cutting board. Take a rolling pin and roll out dough until dough is flattened and long. Cut dough in long 1 inch strips. Place strips on top of peach mixture in checkerboard pattern or pattern of your choice.

Sprinkle white and brown sugar on the top of your crust. Sprinkle a small amount of nutmeg and brown sugar over the top of your crust.

Place cobbler in the oven for 45 minutes on 350 °F.

BRILLIANT BREAD PUDDING WITH BOURBON SAUCE

Ingredients:

1 loaf of day old Bread cut in ½ inch pieces

2 cups White sugar

½ cup Brown sugar

2 ½ cups Milk

8 oz Heavy Whipping Cream

½ tablespoon Vanilla Extract

½ tablespoon Nutmeg

1 tablespoon Cinnamon

2 whole Eggs

1 Egg White

½ cup Butter

½ cup Pecans

Directions:

Preheat oven to 350 °F.

On a cutting board, cut day old bread into ¼ inch to ½ inch pieces.

Melt butter in a pan on the stove on medium heat. After butter is melted, reduce heat to low.

Add white sugar, brown sugar, vanilla extract, cinnamon, nutmeg, and eggs and egg white to butter and whisk for about 2 minutes. Add milk and heavy whipping cream and whisk for 1 minute. In a 13X9 inch baking pan, place bread in the pan. Pour milk mixture over the bread. Sprinkle a handful of brown sugar on the top of bread mixture. Sprinkle 1 cup of pecans on the top of your bread mixture.

Place pan in the refrigerator for 20 minutes. This allows the bread to soak and the flavors will seep into the bread.

Directions Continued:

After bread is done soaking into the mixture, remove the pan from the refrigerator. Place bread pudding in the oven and bake for 40 to 45 minutes on 350 °F. Allow the bread pudding to cool for five minutes before serving.

Bourbon sauce Ingredients:

1 tablespoon bourbon

1 teaspoon vanilla extract

2 cups confectioner's sugar

2 tablespoons butter

2 tablespoons cornstarch

Bourbon Sauce Directions

While the bread pudding is cooling, prepare the bourbon sauce.

Place a small pot on medium heat on the stove. Melt butter. Add confectioner's sugar, vanilla extract, bourbon sauce, and cornstarch and whisk continuously until sauce is to the consistency of your liking.

Pour bourbon sauce on top of bread pudding.

Serve and enjoy.

STUNNING SWEET POTATO PIE

Ingredients:

2 lbs Sweet Potatoes

½ cup Butter

1/2 teaspoon Nutmeg

1 teaspoon Cinnamon

½ cup Marshmallows

3/4 cup Brown Sugar

2 cups White Sugar

2 teaspoons Vanilla Extract

1/8 teaspoon Orange Extract

Ingredients Continued:

1/8 teaspoon Ginger

½ cup Milk (whole or 2%)

½ cup Buttermilk

¼ teaspoon Baking Soda

2 Eggs

1 tablespoon Flour

pinch of Salt

2 (9 inch) Unbaked Pie Crusts

1 quart Water

Directions:

Preheat oven to 350 °F.

Peel Sweet Potatoes.

Fill pot with 1 quart of water and place on medium heat on stove.

Boil potatoes for 35 to 40 minutes or until potatoes are completely soft.

Place hot potatoes into a mixing bowl.

Using a blender, blend out sweet potatoes. While potatoes are hot, add marshmallows to potatoes and blend for about 2 minutes on medium speed with blender.

Add white sugar and brown sugar to the mixing bowl and blend with mixer for about 3 minutes on medium speed.

Place butter into mixing bowl and blend into mixture. Add milk, buttermilk, and eggs to your mixture and blend with mixer. Add cinnamon, nutmeg, ginger, orange extract, and vanilla extract to the mixture and blend with mixer for about 2 minutes.

Add a pinch of salt into your mixture.

Add flour and baking soda to your mixture and blend with mixer for about 30 seconds.

Set mixture aside.

Pour mixture into pie shells. Bake for 45 minutes.

TAMARRAH'S SIGNATURE 6 FLAVOR POUNDCAKE

Ingredients:

3 cups Flour

3 cups Sugar

1 cup Milk

5 Eggs

Pinch Salt

Pinch Baking Soda

Ingredients Continued:

1 teaspoon Baking Powder

½ cup Vegetable Shortening

2 sticks Butter

½ package of Lemon Jell-O Pudding

½ packing of Vanilla Jell-O Pudding

1 ½ teaspoon of each Extract: Vanilla Extract, Almond Extract, Butter Extract, Coconut Extract, Rum Extract, and Lemon Extract

Directions:

Sift three cups of flour and place in large mixing bowl and put aside.

Preheat oven to 350 °F.

Spray a cake bundt pan with non stick baking spray. Take a pinch of flour and spread it around your cake pan. This makes sure that the cake doesn't stick to the pan. Set aside.

Add ½ teaspoon baking powder and a pinch of salt into your flour mixture.

In a separate large bowl, place 3 cups of sugar, ½ cup of vegetable shortening, butter, and milk into the bowl. With an electric mixer, mix the aforementioned ingredients until blended smoothly.

Add 5 eggs to your sugar mixture. Make sure that you add the eggs one at a time. Add one pinch of baking soda, ½ pack of lemon jell-o pudding, and ½ pack of vanilla jell-o pudding into your mixture and blend well with mixer.

Take sifted flour and mix into your sugar mixture. Make sure you mix the flour in a little at a time, until your cake batter is well blended. There should be absolutely "no clumps" in your cake mixture.

Add 1 teaspoon of each extract to your cake mixture. Mix on medium speed for 3 minutes.

Pour cake mixture into cake bundt pan. Bake for 1 hour and 15 minutes or until cake is golden brown and thoroughly cooked at 350 °F.

Remove cake and place in cake dish.

- **Note:** Fill the bundt pan only ½ way because the cake will rise tremendously during baking. This recipe makes 2 average sized bundt cakes.

Ingredients for glaze:

2 tablespoons Butter

¼ cup Water

2 cups Confectioner's Sugar

1 teaspoon of each of the 6 extracts (lemon, almond, rum, coconut, butter, vanilla)

½ Lemon (squeezed juice)

2 tablespoons Corn Starch

1 tablespoon Flour

Directions for Glaze:

Heat stove on high heat.

In a small pot, combine butter, confectioner's sugar, 1 teaspoon of each extract, lemon juice, cornstarch, water, and flour. Mix all ingredients with a large spoon.

When the glaze has a thick consistency, lower the stove's heat.

Allow the glaze to sit for 10 minutes and drizzle on top of your pound cake. Serve and enjoy.

WHO'S FAKE? NO BAKE CHEESECAKE

Ingredients:

½ cup Milk

¼ cup Cool Whip

16 oz Cream Cheese

1 can Pie Filling (Dunkin Hines cherry topping)

1 tsp Vanilla Extract

1 ½ tablespoons Lemon Juice

½ cup Sugar

1 Graham Cracker Pie Crust

<u>Directions:</u>

Place cream cheese in a mixing bowl. On medium speed, soften the cream cheese by mixing for 3 minutes or until cream cheese softens completely.

Add milk, sugar, lemon juice, and vanilla extract to the bowl and blend with mixer for 3 minutes on medium speed.

Add cool whip to mixture and blend well.

Remove the outside covering of your pre made graham cracker crust.

Add cream cheese mixture to the graham cracker crust. With a spatula, smooth out the cream cheese mixture.

Open up cherry pie filling can. Spread pie filling on top of cream cheese mixture.

Cover with plastic top and place in the refrigerator for 4 hours.

Serve.

PRETTY REFRESHING: DRINKS

~ *Vibrant Virgin Strawberry Daiquiri*

~ *Sherbet Delight*

~ *Red Bottom Splash*

~ *Pretty Girl Punch*

~ *Stiletto Lemonade*

DRINKS

There is nothing like consuming a refreshing drink. Drinks can make or break a meal. The type of beverage that you serve with your meal, makes all the difference. Included are some non-alcoholic drinks for any occasion. Also, in this section of the book, you will notice that serving size is included. This allows you to know how many servings the recipe is for. If you need to make more than the serving size listed, double up on the recipe as needed. Cheers!

VIBRANT VIRGIN STRAWBERRY DAIQUIRI

Serving size: This recipe makes 2 servings.

Prep Time: 5 minutes

Ingredients:

12 strawberries

1/2 cup sugar

Ice (3 cups)

1 tablespoon lime juice

1 cup Daiquiri mix

Directions

In a blender, combine strawberries, sugar, daiquiri mix, and lime juice.

Blend until smooth (about 2 minutes on medium speed).

Pour into a sexy or dainty glass and serve.

SHERBET DELIGHT

Serving size: This recipe makes about 10 to 12 (8 oz cups) servings.

Prep Time: 5 minutes

Ingredients:

1.5 Quart Rainbow Sherbet (lime, orange, & pineapple)

4 cups Pineapple juice

1 liter Ginger Ale

Directions:

In a large bowl, combine sherbet, pineapple juice, and ginger ale.

Mix ingredients with a large spoon until all ingredients are combined.

Serve and enjoy!

RED BOTTOM SPLASH

Prep Time: 5 minutes

Serving Size: This recipe makes 2 servings

Ingredients

1/2 cup Orange Juice

1 cup Sprite or Lemon-Lime flavored beverage

2 tablespoons Cherry Grenadine

4 Maraschino Cherries

1/2 cup Pineapple Juice

Directions:

In a pitcher, combine orange juice, sprite, and pineapple juice. Pour mixture into 2 glasses.

Add 1 tablespoon of cherry grenadine to each glass and let grenadine sink to the bottom of the glass.

Add maraschino cherries to drinks. Garnish with fruit of choice.

PRETTY GIRL PUNCH

Prep Time: 5 minutes

Serving Size: This recipe makes 4 servings.

Ingredients:

8 oz Peach Juice

4 oz Pineapple Juice

4 oz Mango Juice

2 tablespoons Cherry Grenadine

Directions:

In a pitcher, mix peach juice, pineapple juice, mango juice, and cherry grenadine. Chill in the refrigerator for 2 hours and serve. Garnish with fruit of choice. Serve and enjoy.

STILETTO LEMONADE

Prep Time: 7 minutes

Serving Size: This recipe makes 4 servings.

Ingredients:

6 cups of Cold Water.

3 cups fresh Lemon Juice

4 cups Sugar

1 8 oz can Dole pineapples (with the juice)

½ teaspoon of Sweet and Sour Mix

Directions:

In a pitcher, mix water, lemon juice, sweet and sour mix, and sugar.

Add pineapples and pineapple juice to the mixture.

Chill in the refrigerator for 2 hours before serving.

APPENDICES

Appendix A: Sample Meal Plans

Appendix B: Entertaining Tips

Appendix C: Basic Kitchen Utensils Needed

APPENDIX A: SAMPLE MEAL PLANS

Planning any meal can be a simple task when preparation is involved. In this appendix, some suggestions for meals are included as a guide to help you with your meal compilation. Meals should contain at least 1 meat, 1 starch, and 1 veggie. You should not have all starches with the main entrée. Also, make sure that your meals have a variety of color. Included are some sample meal plans using the recipes given in this cookbook. These meal plans can serve as a guide and/or blueprint for your meal plan preparation. Take a look ladies and enjoy!!!

Meal Plan #1:

Appetizer: Slamming Salad

Main Entrée: Beautiful Baked Ziti

Dessert: Tamarrah's Signature 6 Flavor Pound cake

Drink: Pretty Girl Punch

*This meal does not have a side dish because the salad can be considered either an appetizer or side dish.

Meal Plan #2

Appetizer: Easy Breezy Meatballs

Main Entrée: Brazing BBQ Chicken

Side Dish: Turn Up Cabbage

Side Dish: Banging Macaroni & Cheese

Dessert: Who's Fake? No Bake Cheesecake

Drink: Stiletto Lemonade

Meal Plan #3

Main Entrée: Jamming Curry Chicken and Shrimp

Side Dish: Turn Up Cabbage

Side Dish: Slap Your Momma Cornbread

Dessert: Prissy Peach Cobbler

Drink: Red Bottom Splash

Meal Plan #4

Main Entrée: Rocking Roast

Side Dish: Wild Out Rice

Side Dish: Boss Baked Beans

Drink: Virgin Strawberry Daiquiri

Dessert: Brazing Bread Pudding with Bourbon Sauce

APPENDIX B: ENTERTAINING TIPS

This section of the book provides entertaining tips to every Pretty Girl. As the host, you want to create a memorable moment for your guests. The ambiance of your location, menu, and décor should resemble your personality, coupled with a touch of grace. Check out my tips for entertaining.

Tip #1

Make a playlist of the respective music that you will be playing during this time. Music is the yin to the yang of any atmosphere. Make sure that the ambiance reflects your personality. When guests come to into your domain, you want to create an ambiance and aura that is inviting, welcoming, and organic. If you are a subtle type of girl, play spa like music to set the atmosphere. If you are a hopeless romantic and you are cooking for your significant other, play some soft jazz or R Kelly. If you are a high spirited type of girl, play some Beyonce' music to get the party started. Whatever you do, make sure that the ambiance is set for the appropriate guest. You would never want to play Young Jeezy if the president were coming over to your house. LOL.

Tip #2

Stage your location. Décor is important. Use candles such as tea lights when preparing an intimate meal. If you are cooking for family, try decorating the dinner table with a few flower centerpieces. If you are hosting a dinner meeting for business, use your best china and glassware. NEVER use plastic plates and cups when entertaining guests.

Tip #3

Maintain consistency. Start with Appetizers. Then serve the main entrée, followed by dessert. Don't serve food out of order.

Tip #4

Make sure your environment and hosting area are clean. Purchase soft scent air fresheners such as lavender and vanilla. Don't use overpowering scents as this will turn off some guests.

Tip #5

Prep early. Cooking can be a daunting task when you don't prepare. Purchase all of your cooking ingredients a day or 2 before you cook. This will reduce your stress. You don't want to do things at the last minute.

Tip #6

Find out ahead of time what guest allergies or food dislikes are. There is nothing more disappointing than having a guest over for dinner who won't eat any of your cooking. Research what your guests like to eat. You want to make their experience in your domain an enjoyable one.

Tip #7

The most important tip is to "Turn Up" (i.e., amp it up a notch) and enjoy yourself. Food brings comfort. Food and people bring joy and comfort. Enjoy the moment. Enjoy your guests. Have fun girls!

APPENDIX C: BASIC KITCHEN UTENSILS NEEDED

Every pretty girl needs the proper culinary tools to make magic happen in the kitchen. The following tools are needed for many of the meals included in this cookbook.

Mixing bowl

Whisk

13x9 inch baking pan

Measuring cups & spoons

Cutting board

Culinary knife (cutting knife)

Crock Pot

Strainer

Wooden Spoon

Kitchen Shears

Durable Skillets & Pans

Circular Cake Pan

Apron

Various sized Skillets

INDEX

A

Acknowledgements, 4

Appendices, 75

Appetizers, 7

B

Banging Macaroni & Cheese, 42

Beautiful Baked Ziti, 44

Beef & Broccoli with Rice, 38

Boss Baked Beans, 44

Bougie Baked Potatoes, 16

Bourbon, 51, 55-56

Brazing BBQ Chicken, 26

Brilliant Bread Pudding, 55, 56

C

Cabbage, 49

Cake, 59, 62

Catch it Spaghetti, 20, 28

Chicken, 11, 25, 26, 34, 36

Chicken Quesadilla, 36

Cornbread, 47

D

Dedication, 3

Desserts, 51, 52

Delectable Sweet Potato Pie, 52, 57

Drinks, 64, 65

E

Easy Breezy Meatballs, 9, 10

Entertaining, 6, 52, 79

Ethnic, 32, 33

F

Flaming Fried Chicken Wings, 11

Flour, 11-12,24,47-48,58-61

I

Introduction, 6

J

Jamming Curry Chicken & Shrimp, 34

M

Main Entrees, 17-18, 32-33, 41, 76-77

Meal Prep, 66, 68, 70-71, 73, 76, 80

Mushroom Chicken with Linguine, 24-25

N

No Bake Cheesecake, 62, 77

P

Peach Cobbler, 51-53, 77

Pretty Girl Punch, 64, 71, 77

Q

Queen's Pie, 17, 30

R

Red Bottom Splash, 70, 77

Rice, 32, 34, 38-41, 46, 48

Rocking Roast, 17, 21-22, 78

S

Salsa, 37

Sassy Sandwiches, 7, 9, 15

Sherbet Delight, 64, 68-69

Side Dishes, 40-41

Slap Your Momma Cornbread, 40, 47-48, 77

Slamming Salad, 7, 13, 77

Smacking Smothered Pork Chops, 17, 23

Spaghetti, 17, 20, 28-29

Stiletto Lemonade, 64, 73, 77

T

Tamarrah's 6 flavor Pound Cake, 51, 61, 77

Turn up Cabbage, 40, 49-50, 77

V

Virgin Strawberry Daiquiri, 64, 66, 78

W

Who's Fake? No Bake Cheesecake, 51, 62, 77

Wild Out Rice, 40, 46, 78

About the Author

      Tamarrah Tarver-Small, PhD is a "Pretty Girl" in her own right. She is truly a Queen of all trades. PhD Tamarrah Tarver-Small is the CEO of Pretty Girl World (PGW). It is an organization that promotes wholeness to every girl. Tamarrah possesses a PhD in Christian Counseling, a Masters degree in Psychology, and a Bachelor's degree in Psychology. Tamarrah has been cooking as far back as she can remember. She was never taught how to cook. It's a gift that Tamarrah feels that she was endowed with from God. Tamarrah did however, take a cooking course in high school that ignited a spark and passion for cooking. While in that cooking class, Tamarrah chose to deviate from the recipes given by the instructor and added a twist to the recipes given. Her food was always magical. From then on Tamarrah knew that she was sort of a natural in the kitchen. Each time Tamarrah prepares a dish people tend to ask for more. The secret behind Tamarrah's recipes is LOVE. Tamarrah loves to cook and she loves watching people enjoy the food that she prepares. Food brings people together. Good food brings people joy. Tamarrah is a pretty girl who wants to inspire pretty girls all over the world to cook her dishes.

Made in the USA
Middletown, DE
26 October 2022

13576114R00051